Healthy Relationships

*Discover How to Build
the 5 Fundamental Pillars
of a Healthy Relationship
with Your Romantic
Partner*

by Leslie Steinburg

Table of Contents

Introduction

Every romantic relationship starts out a little different, and every romantic relationship functions in its own unique way. This is good, because no one wants to be just like everyone else. Yet, even with all these differences, it is important to note that all romantic relationships must have a good, strong foundation in order to remain long-lasting. In this book I've put together a detailed description of the five most important attributes that form the basis of a solid romantic relationship, and because they represent the foundation for which the rest of the relationship must be built upon, I like to refer to each of these attributes as a pillar. It would not be helpful for me to simply list them and leave you to your own devices, however. Therefore, each pillar will be discussed thoroughly in its own chapter, including a detailed description of how that pillar should be put into everyday practice within your relationship.

Refer back to this book at any time, whether you're single, in a new relationship, or well into a long relationship. And if you're wondering why I'd recommend this information to you as a single person, well, it can be a great tool to help you determine whether a potential partner might be a good match for you or not. You can use it to crosscheck their values against your own, and see how well you match up.

Keep in mind that the techniques for implementing these values into your life are merely suggestions, and may not work exactly the same for everyone. If you would like to go about your relationship in a slightly different way, then you can simply modify my advice and adjust it accordingly to better suit your personality and your partner's. Also, please know that as you read and think about your relationship, you may find that you have some areas that need more work than others. And that's perfectly alright! If you can at least begin to identify what needs work, then you're off to an excellent start.

You may also find that, while my own personal five pillars are helpful, they aren't the five pillars that you and your partner would necessarily choose. This is okay too. Even if they only serve as a starting point for you, it is very important that you identify and implement your own personal five pillars. Keep in mind that you are also allowed to have more than five and that they don't necessarily need to be ranked in any order of importance in your mind; you just need to be consciously aware of them with your partner each day in order to make them useful.

An important telltale sign that your relationship may not be destined to work out is if your partner continually thinks that the idea of discussing what is important to you is silly or stupid. It's all right if he or she shows a little bit of trepidation at first; because change – even positive change – can be daunting at first. But if that attitude continues or worsens, then it might be worth considering whether your values still line up, or whether they ever did in the first place. With that said, let me go ahead and list the 5 pillars, which are in no particular order because they're all equally as important: love, trust, communication, intimacy, and integrity.

Let's get started!

Chapter 1: The Pillar of Love

You might think that love is a little bit of a no-brainer. "Why would I be in a romantic relationship with someone I don't love?" But you would be surprised how many couples actually question whether love still remains within their relationship. This can happen for many reason, whether it's due to recent trauma, such as the death of a loved one, a birth, losing a job, or financial loss; it could be a very long relationship that has endured through a lot of life changes, perhaps out of necessity, or a relationship that perhaps started for the wrong reasons (such as a purely sexual basis), in which the partners now find that they actually want it to grow and deepen.

Even if you know in the back of your mind that love does exist in your relationship, maybe it's just that you and your partner have become so used to one another that you have forgotten to actively show it each and every day, or perhaps you have made the all too common mistake of thinking that they don't need you to show it because they already know. Let me get this out in the open now, even if someone is fully aware that you are head over heels in love with them, it is necessary for you to remind and show them. It's a form of reassurance that you should learn to do, because it's much more effective than just saying, "Hey, you know I love you, right?" from time to time.

Of course, this is also something you should probably do, from time to time, but it can't be the only way your partner is ever "told." This act will then just become empty words, and empty words lose their meaning, even if they are sincere. Remember, you aren't in a business relationship with this person; they are your life partner, your husband or wife, or at the very least an incredibly important boyfriend or girlfriend. Think of ways to remind them every single day how important they are to you, and they will begin to follow by doing the same, even if it takes them a little bit to catch on.

You might be wondering what some things are that you can do to show your partner that you love them.

Firstly, use what you know about your partner. And if you don't know a whole lot that should tell you something, it either means that you don't ask them enough questions about themselves or that they are having a hard time opening up to you, which means that you guys probably need to pay extra attention to the chapter on trust, but we'll get to that later. If the reason you don't know a lot about your partner is because the relationship is a new one, then now is a great time to begin asking questions. This also overlaps with the chapter on communication, but here I want to focus more on what you love about them. Do you know what they love about you? Have you made it a point to ask? Have they just told you, or some combination of the two?

Love is expressed by an interest in knowing more about the other person. You'll know whether you have love in your relationship if you know about your partner's childhood. Who is their favorite relative? Favorite pet? Where did they live growing up? What about their best friend? Has it been the same person all their life or did that change? The same questions apply to their favorite food or what they wanted to be when they grew up. Do you know what their proudest or most embarrassing moments were, both as a child and as an adult?

Next, you should ask yourself about your reactions to the things they have told you and the things they love, such as hobbies. Now, as a couple, it's more than likely that you guys have a bunch of common interests. But of course, there are always outliers. I'm sure there were some things that, when you first began dating, you were afraid to reveal to your partner for fear of some kind of judgment, whether of the serious or silly variety, or perhaps a bit of both. Ask yourself, are you still afraid to reveal these things to your partner (especially if you have been in a relationship for a while now)? If the answer is yes, then you might want to evaluate why that is. Is it your own personal fears holding you back? Or do you fear that their love for you might diminish or change in a way you won't like? If you find that the answer is the second one, then ask yourself whether you at least feel comfortable enough with your partner to address why that might be something you struggle with. If you aren't even comfortable doing that, then you should probably reevaluate your relationship in its entirety.

Now let's flip that entire set of questions you posed to yourself on its head. If you have fears and/or doubts about revealing something about yourself to your partner, then it's extremely likely that they also have some fears as well. When you go to talk to them about things that are difficult for you to reveal, you should ask them whether they have something similar they would like to talk to you about. Establish whether and why you both have this fear, and you've got a healthy starting point towards regenerating the love in your relationship.

And remember, in order to show love you should always:

- Say "I love you." (but do it when it's important/when you mean it)

- Kiss.

- Be otherwise physically affectionate, such as with holding hands, brushing each other's arms, playing with hair, hugging, cuddling, or putting your arm around their shoulders or waist.

- Ask them questions about themselves as you both grow as people. (because remember, we all change)

- Ask about their day.

- Ask about the things they read and their hobbies.

Never outright dismiss those hobbies and interests, nor any ideas that they might have. If you find yourself constantly thinking that what your partner has to do or wants to say is stupid, then you need to reevaluate. To get out of this habit, try giving them the benefit of the doubt. You may actually discover that you like what you find, and that your partner

11

has actually taught you something new. And it's a sure sign of rekindling love if you find yourself learning something new from your partner or being influenced by them in some way every day. The influence doesn't need to be anything huge; it could just be that they wanted to show you an artist or a band or a movie, and you actually enjoyed it.

Once these changes begin to happen, you are well on your way to having a love-filled relationship.

Chapter 2: The Pillar of Trust

Trust is absolutely integral to a good relationship, and it can be the hardest component to rebuild once lost. Trust relies on a lot of other things to be built up properly, such as a foundation in love and communication. In fact, if you ask each other the questions and do the exercises that I mentioned in the chapter on love, you will definitely build up trust.

Aside from learning as much as you can about each other, you must also learn to confide in each other. Just as you never would have tattled on or told others your best friend's secrets in elementary school, it's important not to betray the trust of your partner. Now of course, this cannot be held up if you find that they are doing something unethical or immoral, but in general, if your partner is trustworthy, then you should not betray their trust. And yes, this includes informing your best friend. If you are ever unsure whether what your partner told you was in confidence or not, go the safe route and don't tell anyone else until you have cleared up the confusion with them.

Trust is based on little things which build up to big things, so keep the little promises that you make. From experience, I know that nothing wears down trust as fast as a partner who always says they're going to call on break but never does. And it doesn't matter that you had, in your head, a good reason for not calling, such as not wanting to disturb that person or wake them up. If you've told your partner that you'd call and they'd agreed, then call. The same is true for if you said you'd bring home dinner, run an errand, etc. One episode of forgetfulness every so often is no big deal, but don't let not doing these little things become a habit, because then you'll have a bigger problem.

If your partner trusts you with the little things, then it's very likely that they'll trust you with bigger things, such as financial responsibility or staying faithful to them.

However, if you are in a new relationship and your partner already has trust issues even before you had a chance to mess up and/or prove yourself, be aware that that is not your cross to bear alone. Trust issues can be something that can wreck a relationship if left unchecked, but you shouldn't immediately ditch a relationship if they come to light because that won't help your partner heal. Instead, see if your partner is open to seeking the help of a therapist to work through some of their issues together with you.

Physical interaction can also help build trust as well, and this is something that I learned from my many years in theatre. Try doing physical activities with your partner, whether it be a theatre workshop, in which you will learn how to take physical cues from one another, maintain and communicate with each other via eye contact, and you might even learn to do something called a trust fall, which can be quite scary at first but is fun once you get used to it, much like a romantic relationship.

But what happens to all that trust if you do happen to make a mistake? Well, we're all human, and everyone is bound to mess up once in a while. It might be a little or a big mess, but both you and your partner will end up making one. That doesn't automatically mean that all trust is extinguished just like that. In order to reestablish and maintain that chain of trust, you must apologize sincerely. And just saying the words, "I'm sorry" isn't good enough. In order for an apology to be effective, you must take responsibility for whatever it is that you've done wrong and do your best to ensure that it won't ever happen again.

Keep in mind that while you are rebuilding trust and proving that you can make that positive change, you may have to reassure your partner quite often and do little things consciously in order to make up for it and reform their basis for trust. While this is all right and to be expected, keep in mind that it will also be necessary for your partner to let go of whatever has happened and learn to forgive and trust you again. Even if you are the one to mess up, you should not still have to be paying for a mistake several months down the road. It takes both people in the relationship to keep the trust alive.

As you build your trustworthiness again, be aware that all the pillars in this book are intertwined, and depend on one another to keep the relationship alive and well.

Chapter 3:   The   Pillar   of
Communication

Communication is key to any romantic relationship, and a loss of communication can mean the death of it. Communication does not always have to involve words, although that is a big part of it. And the most important thing to know about communication in a relationship is not *how to* do it, but how to do it *effectively* for yourself and your partner, since everyone communicates a little bit differently. Always keep in mind that the end goal is to be clear and honest, never confusing or deceiving.

A big misconception about communication is that it's all about talking, but in actuality, it's more about listening. If you find yourself in a situation where you are doing all the talking, then you probably are not communicating very effectively with your partner. Conversation should be more of an exchange; no one person should monopolize the entire conversation, and no one should feel as though they are talking to a wall. Yet again, listening does not just mean allowing your partner to speak. If it's going in one ear and out the other, then it's no use to either one of you. Make sure that you are listening and actually hearing what the other person is saying in order to respond the most effectively. And while trying to talk, especially about something important, don't feel like you have to fill all of the empty space. Silence can be a good thing; it means that either you or your partner are genuinely stopping and reflecting on how to respond to something you've been told.

Going back to my theatre training again, I'd like to say that it's very important to be there with your partner as they're speaking to you. No, I don't necessarily mean physically, but to be emotionally and mentally "there" and engaged. This will also help you in my above tip of listening. Focus on how they look as they're standing or sitting in front of you. Notice the situations going on around you and how they are reacting, if that's relevant to the conversation. Your partner will be able to tell that you are truly engaged and that you care about what they're saying. I have found that this can also help to fend off arguments, because a lot of arguments begin with a segue of: "You aren't listening to me." If you *are* listening, this is very unlikely to happen. Also, if you stay focused in the moment, you are less likely to argue about things that have previously happened. You can stay focused on the subject and conversation at hand.

Plus, the more you pay attention, the more you will be able to pick up physical, nonverbal cues, which can often tell you more than just words alone. Just some basics, for example, are: if a person is angled towards you and has left their chest open, it means that they are open and receptive to the conversation. If they have their arms crossed over their chest, it may mean that they are either uncomfortable or angry. If they are sitting closer to you, they are receptive, if they keep getting further and further away, it isn't a good sign.

Use all of these tips to help make communication with your partner more effective, and remember, it's more about attentive listening than talking.

Chapter 4: The Pillar of Intimacy

Since we are discussing romantic relationships within the scope of this book, intimacy is inclusive of both sexual and non-sexual forms, and both are very important. Let's start with talking about sexual intimacy.

This can be a scary subject, even for a lot of very committed, caring couples. Odds are, if you have a fulfilling sex life, then both you and your partner are very open and communicative about what the other wants and needs. As I said before, all the pillars of a good romantic relationship are intertwined with one another, they depend upon each other; so when speaking about sexual intimacy within your relationship, you should use your newly acquired communication and trust skills.

Trust can also affect your sex life; if your partner doesn't trust you in other aspects of life, it's possible they won't trust you in sex, and the same goes for you. If you don't have a very adventurous sex life to begin with, it might be wise to build up that trust in intimacy and thus build up to what you will do in the bedroom, rather than jumping in headfirst without knowing where you're going.

You should discuss your sex life as it is at present, and find out what your partner is satisfied with and what needs work. After that's been opened up, discuss your needs and their needs, see what overlaps and what differs. When you go into trying something new, take baby steps, and always make sure that you have a safe word, in case either you or your partner feels too overwhelmed by a certain act or the pace of things. Always be open, honest, and caring with one another, and after you have tried something new, check up with each other and take care of each other emotionally. You never want a new sexual experience or experiment to lead to trauma or distrust, you want it to lead to a growing closeness and trustfulness.

Now, what about non-sexual intimacy? This is just as important, if not more so, because it can actually help to build up your intimacy in the bedroom. Intimacy comes with sharing important details about yourself, which in turn denotes trust. Talk with your partner about the things that mean a lot to you, about your achievements, your goals, and your failures. Entrust them with details about yourself that perhaps not even your mother or your best friend knows about you. This will make them feel trusted and special.

Intimacy can also come from the little daily tasks the two of you do together, be it making meals, walking the dog, or brushing your teeth. You may not think that any of these things are inherently sexy, and you'd be right; but when you've signed up for a committed relationship, it then becomes your job, of sorts, to inject that loving sexiness into those everyday acts. This is what makes them intimate. It's as simple as the brush of an arm when you pass your hubby the eggs to pour into the pan, or eye contact as you both spit into the sink, or laughing until you ache as your tiny dog chases after a squirrel. These moments can be intimate with the right body language, and if you choose to think of them as such.

Chapter 5: The Pillar of Integrity

Integrity is defined as being a person who has strong moral principles or who is morally upright. Now, when I mention morality, don't assume that this necessarily means that you need to be religious, because that isn't the case at all. Today, people can have differing moral codes that are all very valid as long as they include the following: trustworthiness, honesty, forthrightness, openness, and love for people around you. Fortunately, these are all the things that I've mentioned in previous chapters that you need in order to have a successful relationship with your partner. If you do all of those things, you will then become a person of integrity.

Integrity is something that a lot of other people can vouch for as well. These include friends, family members, and sometimes even complete strangers. If you have a good track record with other people in your life, chances are that it is going to carry over into your relationship. If something in your relationship ever has you questioning your own personal integrity, then you should investigate whether it's you who has actually changed or if it's something your partner may be doing. If you have changed or are changing, ask yourself whether it's a change that you can live with. If not, then reevaluate. To me, the pillar of integrity is when it comes down to staying true to yourself while also being within your relationship.

Some ways to be sure that you are maintaining your integrity are:

- Checking in with yourself. Are you happy with the person you've become while you've been in this relationship? Why or why not?

- Have you grown as a person during this relationship thus far?

- Do people think you have generally stayed the same, or that you have changed for the better?

- Do you feel confined in any way, or do you feel freer?

- Do your family and friends generally approve of your partner/relationship? Is it important that they do?

If you are able to answer all or most of these questions to your satisfaction, then you seem to have a relationship with a lot of integrity. If not, ask yourself if and how the things that seem wrong can be rectified.

Conclusion

In conclusion, I feel that the five pillars of a good relationship can be used at any point in a relationship, new or old, to rekindle it or to keep it going nice and strong. Remember that they are: love, trust, communication, intimacy and integrity, and that all of them are intertwined. You really cannot have one without the other four. But since they all balance and interact with each other, I find that they all flow naturally together.

You and your partner may find that one is more difficult than the other four, and that is fine, as long as you are able to identify where the problem lies and take steps to solve it. This honesty and willingness to work on things already shows that your relationship is strong and worthy of standing tall just as the pillars of a healthy relationship do.

You can also use the pillars to evaluate whether or not a relationship is healthy and whether you want to stay involved in it or not, or even whether a prospective partner is healthy for you.

Keep in mind as you work on your pillars that everyone communicates just a little differently, and that it might be necessary for you to adjust the way in which you communicate in order for the changes implemented in your relationship to be the most effective.

As long as you and your partner both feel a desire to heal and improve your relationship, you are on the right track to have a healthy one.

Finally, I'd like to thank you for purchasing this book! If you found it helpful, I'd greatly appreciate it if you'd take a moment to leave a review on Amazon. Thank you!

Printed in Great Britain
by Amazon

43882517R10030